the operating system print//document

ISBN: 978-1-946031-43-3
Library of Congress Control Number: 2018968369
copyright © 2019 Lori Anderson Moseman
edited and designed by ELÆ [Lynne DeSilva-Johnson]

is released under a Creative Commons CC-BY-NC-ND (Attribution, Non Commercial, No Derivatives) License: its reproduction is encouraged for those who otherwise could not afford its purchase in the case of academic, personal, and other creative usage from which no profit will accrue.

Complete rules and restrictions are available at:
http://creativecommons.org/licenses/by-nc-nd/3.0/

For additional questions regarding reproduction, quotation, or to request a pdf for review contact operator@theoperatingsystem.org

Books from The Operating System are distributed to the trade by SPD/Small Press Distribution, with ePub and POD via Ingram, with production by Spencer Printing, in Honesdale, PA, in the USA.

This text was set in Earwig Factory, Freight Neo Pro, Minion, Franchise, and OCR-A Standard.

Cover Art: digital collage by ELÆ using details of an illustration by Caits Meissner.
Used with permission of the artists.

[Cover Image Description: Composite image with title and author's name in red, boxed, irregular type mimicking found letters, over black and white abstracted hand-drawn dystopian landscape depicting outsized molars, refuse, and fragmented automobiles.]

the operating system
www.theoperatingsystem.org
mailto: operator@theoperatingsystem.org

LORI ANDERSON MOSEMAN

2018-19 OS System Operators

CREATIVE DIRECTOR/FOUNDER/MANAGING EDITOR: ELÆ [Lynne DeSilva-Johnson]
DEPUTY EDITOR: Peter Milne Greiner
CONTRIBUTING EDITOR, EXPERIMENTAL SPECULATIVE POETICS: Kenning JP Garcia
CONTRIBUTING EDITOR, FIELD NOTES: Adrian Silbernagel
CONTRIBUTING EDITOR, IN CORPORE SANO: Amanda Glassman
CONTRIBUTING EDITOR, GLOSSARIUM: Ashkan Eslami Fard
CONTRIBUTING EDITOR, GLOSSARIUM / RESOURCE COORDINATOR: Bahaar Ahsan
JOURNEYHUMAN / SYSTEMS APPRENTICE: Anna Winham
ASSISTANT EDITOR / ACCESSIBILITY MANAGER: Sarah Dougherty
DIGITAL CHAPBOOKS / POETRY MONTH COORDINATOR: Robert Balun
TYPOGRAPHY WRANGLER / DEVELOPMENT COORDINATOR: Zoe Guttenplan
DESIGN ASSISTANTS: Lori Anderson Moseman, Orchid Tierney, Michael Flatt
SOCIAL SYSTEMS / HEALING TECH: Curtis Emery
VOLUNTEERS and/or ADVISORS: Adra Raine, Alexis Quinlan, Clarinda McLow, Bill Considine, Careen Shannon, Joanna C. Valente, L. Ann Wheeler, Jacq Greyja, Erick Sáenz, Knar Gavin, Joe Cogen

The Operating System is a member of the **Radical Open Access Collective**, a community of scholar-led, not-for-profit presses, journals and other open access projects. Now consisting of 40 members, we promote a progressive vision for open publishing in the humanities and social sciences.

Learn more at: http://radicaloa.disruptivemedia.org.uk/about/

Your donation makes our publications, platform and programs possible! We <3 You.
bit.ly/growtheoperatingsystem

Y, a character you too can play 13
body politic | election blues 14
floating infrastructure provides on-demand bridges 15
to be "in the loop" Y steals words of others 16
Y refuses to stop believing in humor's ripple effect 17
hooping Y learns what to do with arms in the current reign 18
Y waits with the nation for an impeachment speech 19
lament this endless rush 20
life jacket made of sleeves torn from cloaks 21
Y tries equalizing country without robots 22
old formulas + hoop lessons 23
pilot boats on the mouth of a river entertain brew masters 24
Y's reading life needs a nightlight 25

beloveds

29		rigor mortis sets in before impeachment
29	i.	prolouge
30	ii.	preamble
31	iii.	six jobs
32	iv.	collapse
33	v.	sick leave
34	vi.	shopping
35	vii.	after snowmelt
36	viii.	phenology at gatehouse
37	ix.	somatic trick
38	x.	tenor terror tender
39	xi.	droid sans
41	xii.	blessings begin

backstories

light corp's wall-o-food offers smart city hope   45
cornucopia   46
(w)hoop into the sky the museum is   47
Y's dumb phone talks back   50
Y = And = I walk, you walk, we walk con un traductor robot   53

notes   62
other works pondered   67
acknowledgements   68

indeterminate   variable   **Y**   unwise   wild   card
curio   catalyst   just   another   organism   in   the   waste   stream
a tracing of analogy-n-ratio as if relation were the life blood of spent fuel rods

Y, a character you too can play

Rusty's spine is wasting away so she tries to hula
hoop to build marrow: she swoops hips to and fro
elbows bent fists clenched gut pushing the inner loop

because rust is the longest war peacenik Rusty banishes
"R-u-s-t" from her name to become the letter *Y*: italic
12 point Minion emerges as her signature size-n-font

in public *Y* tries to slow her mind-n-mouth (damn
speedy gyre) 'cause her time left on this planet is a lot
less than humanity's (duh) partial mortal flourishing

spins a lot like feuding parties within a fixed radius
battering bodies at banter speed like houses of congress
witnesses in a cloud of shame the nation has yet to claim

body politic | election blues

spine a rusted anchor
waist a corroding surge
playful tale this outpouring
contintuum of sewer pipes

Y's hoop begs each vote
to count belly hip oops hear it
hula clatter as Y stoops scoops
loop up knocks it down again

a nothing spin

posing as prayer as pledge
of allegiance to peaceful
transfer of power
the heart of us wage-worn

protest heel-toes toward hope
strong core but
salt belt rust belt outcast coasts
russians hack their way in

a nothing win

promises to restore marrow
but no insuring health now
a contentious brittle crown
that chain of executive orders

never was Y's fault   nor yours
surely Lady Liberty still loves us
as that crude president's pen
guts human rights right out

floating infrastructure provides on-demand bridges

elsewhere:
*robot "pigs"
inspect
pipelines*

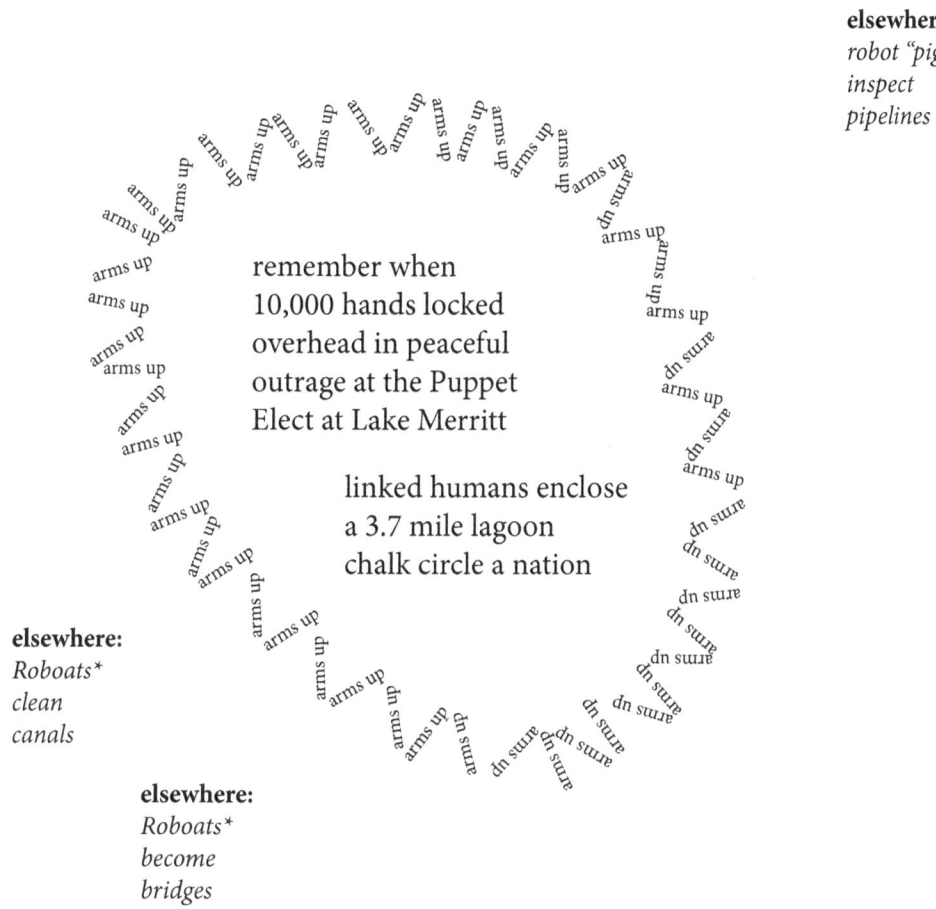

remember when
10,000 hands locked
overhead in peaceful
outrage at the Puppet
Elect at Lake Merritt

linked humans enclose
a 3.7 mile lagoon
chalk circle a nation

elsewhere:
Roboats
clean
canals*

elsewhere:
Roboats
become
bridges*

to be "in the loop" Y steals words of others

if *in the loop* is "to know is an extreme condition"
then its corrosion = connection

if *in the loop* is "the aperture shut tight"
then quality light is that which the excluded bring to bear

if *in the loop* is "a fire and fury like the world has never seen"
then diplomacy is no longer a working barter

if *in the loop* is "locked and loaded"
then folks need to jump out of this bounding game

if the "celebrated vat against time" is not
a "what if" then how can Y be "held for known"

Y refuses to stop believing in humor's ripple effect

imagination begins its hunger strike with no-carry laws
no sticks no shields nothing that uses bullets no pepper
spray or acid or tasers no knifes no cars just hula hoops
yes everyone in Liberty Square gets a hoop cops neo-nazis
antifa clergy medics journalists all get a little free-speech
corral in which to chant or pray or recite the Bill of Rights
hell recalculate taxes just don't lasso your neighbor no
lynching no beating no defamation allowed only contact
permitted is the toy hoop banging your own gut knees calves
chest hips swoop up down don't need to be in sync
to wire neural nets that bridge a divide let's cohabitate
and divvy up food shelter water jobs land and purpose
when we tire we can sit in our grounded halos and wait
for extreme winds to eat away at all our misgivings

hooping Y learns what to do with arms in the current reign

in dead winter Y curls toes so body is a "J" and hoop is an "O"

by spring Y rasies arms in a "V" to reshape body as a "Y"

but exercised J-O-Y proves not to be enough to cast spells

summer drought dries a brittle regime demands a lasoo

Y circles right arm overhead whooping loudly to jack up the hula

now Y needs a lairat and knot lessons so as to hog-tie the kingpin

but a single body is not enough

Y begs her beloveds for an algorithm to change the nation

human history offers no solace: progress begets barbarism

so says *Straw Dogs* and *The Silence of Animals* that preache ire

rangy bureaucracy (yippy ki-yay) slows the unfolding collapse

Y waits with the nation for an impeachment speech

old hips swoop a hula hoop into a slow whir
wheeling a sacral blur about a crumbling frame

then comes the hurricanes
if only a single soul could counter-spin wind speed

if only climate change were a hoax by an educated elite
if only Houston's soon-to-be crushed waterlogged autos

could float chain-linked into bridge upon which citizens
could haul food to Puerto Rico and the Virgin Islands

if only citrus growers of Florida could save their trees
but rust joins every revolution and mold does too

collective abuse makes this planet too hot to cool its jets
to survive all singularity we must join a citizen navy

be certified as health caregivers who harvest seaweed
before North Korea syncs missiles with every tweet

lament this endless rush

       wind's flight flips raft   beloved is the first dumped
       all bodies go under torrent   no up no down just rush
       heart pumping to orient   slap hands here this is the hull
       feel with me for promised air   grope underbelly to find edge
       beloved my mouth can't open   lungs hold on gasp here grasp
       must find gunwale heave   up into air to see oarsman fling
       another body on board not beloved   life raft flips all again
       rushes down street's stream   submerged dumpster snags
       beloved pushed further under   hull careens over bodies again
       forget the boat try dead man float   ease belly up ride tidal
       crest until a bald cypress bares roots cling there
       where the uprooted harbors   debris our only safe house
       buoyancy our only recourse   our bodies pulsing to live

life jacket made of sleeves torn from cloaks

Y collects dental detritus spit-shines
discarded wedges & bloody matrix bands
to jazz up a sagging loop torn from life
jackets so a tiny tooth ring can pretend
to be a boom that sops oil spills so scale
shifts rattle teeth   crowns did you know
get irradiated more than tomatoes
Y wants to sew such radioactive
half-lives of porcelain molar caps onto
plastered canvas with beeswax-n-thread
if only toxicity could be contained
with textiles or text then collaboration
even if imaginary might free *Y* from buying
miles of irrigation tubing to cut-n-sell
as sacred hoops at pipeline roundups

Y tries equalizing country without robots

Y walks two mutts trying a climber's anchor
as a trick to get each to tug equally
droops a cord between each harness-hook
pulls all strands into a central point
ties an infinity knot then clips a carabiner

alas neither dog is a stone: the moving fulcrum remains akimbo

so *Y* makes a homology map with "chromosome-specific
painting probes from the 22 human autosomes
plus the X and Y sex chromosomes"
Y charts "hybridized onto metaphases of normal dog and red fox"
in hopes of engineering equity

invariably the curs — each to own extent — tug *Y* home

this is why *Y* gets a hula-hoop bigger than any waist could spin
places it flat on the ground
arms spread in a "V" legs stacked together in a single "I"
Y naps so any drone could see her as a peace sign

mutts — still hardwired — sound "invader" alert

old formulas + hoop lessons

still hooping as if that could bend
Putin-mentored power Y tries
to partition political correctness
as if curation were a democracy
Y fails and so resorts to Euhler
his ladder insists strength resides
in the bottom rungs this is not
equity but there is a power base
that acts like abacists + algorists
as if inference build proofs w/o us

if hoop is on hips
move hips
if hoop slips jack-it up
with a quick flick
transfer any keening
to the hoop
remember rungs
of a ladder do not move
up or down

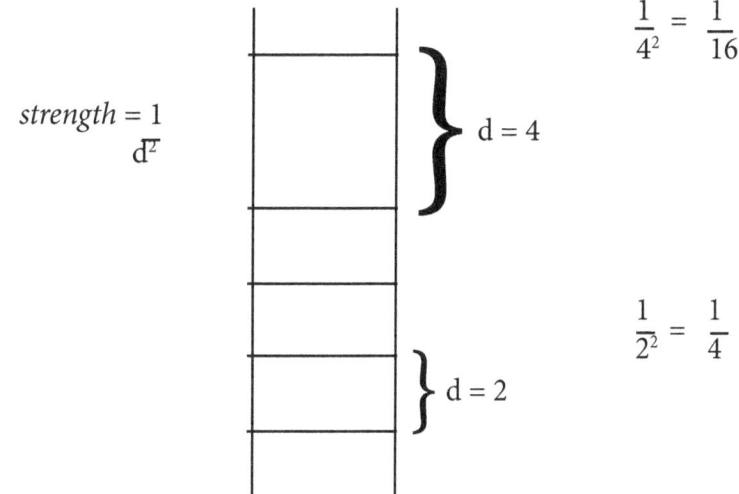

$strength = \dfrac{1}{d^2}$

$\dfrac{1}{4^2} = \dfrac{1}{16}$

$d = 4$

$\dfrac{1}{2^2} = \dfrac{1}{4}$

$d = 2$

pilot boats on the mouth of a river entertain brew masters

        imagine between   mid-latitude

cyclones

                coast lines

    astoria   slash burning 1977

    1922 fire rids city of KKK   start of a work life

                              gas torch and shovel

    labor movements offer

    care of a family   side by side with convict crew

                              filet knife in cannery by night

          guard

sun

        the fishing boat for gathering urchins

        that rode tsunami tides west

water tight

        grounded two years after Fukushima

        dislplayed with a hurricane simulator

                              Kathlamet canoe

        the mouth of a river known for shipwrecks

        the daring of bar pilots

vowels

Y's reading life needs a nightlight

departure
Y mulls dull moments where mathematicians keep calculating
because framework's evident flaws are unprovable   circularity
never make Y abandon

complicated combinations
someday some beloved tweaks a paradox earns an exit
in a context "so far from obvious" answers a problem
Y's hoop never claims

to perfect repeatable curves
not solvable by radicals *Y* likes the method of exhaustion
applied by Archimedes a "bizarre, unmotivated sequence"
not just any spin is

biological necessity
of parallel continuous motions the "split split split split second
after" a kind of parsed spit that lends itself to stanzas
dead sooner than thought

blame

atmospheric drag

a miscalculation

that geo graveyard belt

all of us   **beloveds**   she he they
all of us here now calculating the last arc of this reign
swallowing fear as if the alphabet were vitamins

rigor mortis sets in before impeachment

i. prologue

beloved cannot swallow —
    gut too distended to be recognized

emergency MRI readers guess
    "obstruction is the body itself"

butt-n-throat scopes can't calm
    buckling pain before or after

tubes funnel food through nose
    suction pumps acids out naval

later beloved gets chest hammered
    for three code blues Y screams

holding corpse's hand as wrist's
    barcode gets scanned — a signal

pulse's need for prompt transport
    gone careful calculation eats away

hope slowly at first then faster
    in a feast of many empty tables

ii.   ***preamble***

         here's where all beloveds — we and they —
         weep to lose the belief democracy is
         a solvable problem   we and they speed-
         dial representatives grilling nepotism's
         appointed rich ranters-n-ranchers
         so anticipated suffering becomes
         momentum loud enough to drown-out
         food bank volunteers sorting dented
         cans in donation's bin   here's where
         gut bacteria plus genetic make-up
         plus auras from microbial colonies
         summons bodily fluids as if hyperobjects
         jack-knifed like culverts midstream —
         planet's rivers quench us then drag us

iii. six jobs

beloved itinerant chef dreams of a farm
but has no bed and must walk between six jobs
napping a breakroom couch while POTUS'
campaign guru launders 75 million
so the orange one can promise to make pipe
"like in the old days"   another beloved
replaces lead-laced cast iron sewer lines
with thermoplastic tubes less dependent
on crude... still corruption eats middle rungs
of our national ladder forcing Rusty Justice —
that excavator extraordinaire — to train
coal miners to code for tech-savvy solar
dealers leaving debris removal start-ups
racing the tropics to find houses blown to bits

iv. collapse

        beloved uses both arms to push off the sofa
        swings both legs in tandem a parallel strut
        feet plant firmly on the floor
        fibula   tibia   brittle pipes buckle
        under the weight of the upright
        inordinate pain   can't you hear it
        legs bust
        bad nutrition a pre-existing condition
        beloved crawls to out-maneuver federalist
        papers simplifying allowable permutations

v. sick leave

beloved teaches kayaking to veterans altered by IEDs
chucks her bucket list for a menu of risk aversion
notes drones that should never enter a mouth:

— robot pigs that cleans Dakota Access pipelines
— 10-hour bot lasts only 3 hours in Fukushima's crippled reactor
— LA-tested autonomous car destined to die in a NOLA pothole

beloved agrees some toxic agents are acceptable:

— barium laced chocolate milk illuminating inflamed kidneys
— laser wand trained to cure porcelain plugging decayed incisors
— magnets designed to clamp a subversive jaw shut

beloved dreams of designing robotic suit for paraplegics

vi. shopping

      supermarket's outer ring harbors
      milk that contains no milk —
      no inner circle within the frozen aisle

      cooperating amid mini and maxi carts
      beloved maintains kindness is a hand-basket
      an emptiness wheeling about

      as singular as a vote not counted
      in the electoral college beloved's kale
      does not trump neighbors' tomato tins

      all share bacteria by merely breathing
      in a congenial conversation though they never
      sup together around beloved's family's table

      where humor mounds into story problem
      her mother cannot solve because she smells a rat
      "you're the same rancid as your father"

vii. after snowmelt

ground so brown beloved must paint interior space artic white
grinds wire brush round a corroded wrought iron table

rust — ancient as pollen — floats dust under birch's catkins
before paint dries as engineered to look hammered

magnolias bud without lament without patent
leathery leaves eat each day's very hot sunbeams

doc's digital calipers stop measuring cystic ovaries
don't care whose birth/death their increments serve

beloved asks: what if Zion never counts the zillion pilgrims
waiting at tollbooths while the nation's elite blames the schism

on willing gawkers cocking necks in awe at sheer faces
at pounds of pressure compress — eons without angst

viii. phenology at gatehouse

beloved stops looking for alphabet of self monitors
and opens to simple binaries by collecting data

Y N circle one: leaf buds open?
Y N circle one: leaf?
Y N circle one: flower bud?
Y N circle one: flower bud open?

apple cedar rust gall on a reference tree
of no import for citizen scientists assigned
to monitor the same seven trees   Y N

if the nation does not manage for disease
preserves the Preserve policy of letting
nature take its course then risk is a halo
assigned to each being born   Y N

life altering laments supplant checklists   Y N

ix. somatic trick

        diffuse sunrays filter through canopy
beloved tastes bear breath, fingers fern stoma
           finds the underbelly of exchange
   trading trees for rock, beloved enters Zion

the canyon is a bathtub the body cannot get out of

        not by wingsuit and careful calculation
not by hirsute mortification even if awe were
a path and math were a chant no way for bones
to exit earth's equations   wind-n-water collaborate

x. tenor terror tender

        out the new window
        one yellow leaf is left hanging until
        beloved leans
        forward to find another
        branch hosting fifteen golden hold-outs
        teeth of their umber edge
        imperceptible
        at this distance
        beloveds sits
        so birch's trunk obliterates
        a rusted pole that holds
        a backboard facing the way beloved faces
        quiet
        aloof
        no net   no ball below
        no frantic thrashing   no thighs
        contracting to leap   arc
        back behind this Word window
        a screen saver
        solo hike in a canyon
        beloved beheld
        one sunrise

xi. droid sans

the sassy stubby leg
of the lower case "d" kicks
beloved's burgeoning fear
of an android takeover.
the font industry pesters
each reader, fosters a faux
need to navigate digital
interfaces with panache.
so we vet each pastoral
in Submittable and Dropbox;
any ditty that earns a début
via an interweb journal,
must promptly be converted
into a teaser for Instagram.
we applaud the legibility
of consistently sculpted
alphabet. a pioneer in html
zines, beloved now longs not
to thin Douglas-fir again
to help deplete fuel
in the fire-laden west but
to retool as a forest therapist
who can work anywhere
regeneration is still possible.
why not teach screen-centric
souls stuck on ornamental tuft

the joy of duff's microbes (ticks
and all)? hell, the author
of *Cyborg Manifesto* now touts
companion species, barking:
"shut up and train" to devotees
who seek "partial mortal
flourishing." literary immortality
amid planetary collapse
is vital coifed prayer.
still, the dominant male
amber eyes and reactivity
persist. climate political
lovers shot down in Vegas
damn near a hundred.
we knew circling prey
but did not know just how
shallow an arc
a week before the massacre.
wolf experts shouts orders:
Y turns pivots redirects
walks away. hounds all
hardwired to protect?
pack persists in cutting tax
adding to our demise

xii. blessings begin

with an upright piano
its mechanisms exposed
beloveds are felt
hammers pounding
vibrating wires
tuned to collaborate

beloveds are keys
outnumbering fingers
agile flitting
noted   measured
as if sawdust
from a hollowing

a resonating a path
pulse soothes skin's
cracks bounds
sounds a temple anew
go ahead baby
outgrow your shoe

backstories

colony   working
against   collapse   still   paying   rent   here   concurrent   caring   a   shelter
in   this   constant   summer   where   polymaths   and   mulivocals   exchange   more

light corp's wall-o-food offers smart city hope

Now that "light recipies improve vertical farms' crop yields," the bulb corporation profits from precision farming and Pew Charitable Trust sends each homeowner a slick mag to brag that "knowledge" plus "purpose" has created "a new age of invention."

Because more is better and warehouse hydroponic fields are weather-free, "uniform illumination of tailor-made light provides consistency" that will feed the projected 9.6 billion mouths that will grace the planet in 2050.

Y is dubious and skips lunch to trace alliteration and acroymns populating the propaganda: the promised transformed farming footprint will come from increased food, feed, fiber, and fuel. VRT and UAV will join GPS to speed up seeders, spreaders, and sprayers on traditional farms. Bird's-eye view and wavelength monitors will allow site-specific crop management.

In the blissful moments before the robot uprising, savvy ag specialists who can fix sensors and fly drones will figure out spatial data analysis so field worker and famers will feel less fatique after these *Trends* come to light up our lives in cement bunkers on designated high ground.

cornucopia

"Hey kindred," Y bows to every brittle crown rustling along the oak-lined carriage road. The season for tree rings to pile upon themselves is over, and russet crowns release less fresh air. The watchtower's new clay roof a burnt umber. Camouflage a false comfort: corrosion cannot hide its lust for oxygen. Rust, have you read, is the longest war: "More damning than natural disasters…. corroding pipes everywhere." Every toxin," Y thinks, exits its assigned system. All a toxic target.

Exit our national system? How? Not by a leisurely walk in a nature preserve. in the aftermath of the well-fed, Y needs a cafeteria shift: eight hours, minimum wage w/ a new fangled stainless steel Conserver XL-E dish machine low temp no waste water. Or apple-picking. No. A food bank! Lightened by the promises to serve, Y chats with the cop who slaps two parking tickets on Y's car.

Next week, in route the food distribution warehouse, Y stops at Global Oil's storage facility to crawl inside rusting pipe 25-feet in diameter. Y's hula hoop, a tiny circle inside this cylinder, sounds timid, even tinney as it clatters down. Try again. Six revolutions, seven revolutions, eight revolutions. How many will it take to drown out the residue neoliberal echo chamber all their Facebook clickbacks have etched in Y's frontal lobe?

Post-election grief subsides an hour later as Y dips her torso into a bin full of store-donated food. Check dents. Check inner seals. Check expiration dates. Sort cookie mix, Halloween cereal, strawberry milk, gummy bears. No soup. No beans. Just soda pop. Y chatters: "The author of *Rust* says, 'no woman should eat canned food.'" Workers discuss epoxy liners, sugar's corrosive power, while divvying up toxic food to share to those who have none.

(w)hoop into the sky the museum is

Step into the hoop or drop it overhead? Y hovers outside the art museum near the empty coat rack then opts to lower the plastic halo over a new hair cut, letting the hula tube's blinking lights bless the smart bob. Y's hands hold the child's toy level a fist-length below each hip, keeping long arms slack. Luckily, the grand glass door has a handicap button Y can push with an elbow. Tuesday's docent, who had been forewarned, nods as Y enters.

Once in the reified space, an imp of the perverse leads Y on a path not planned: walking counter-clockwise around Baker's "The Circle of Change" four times, Y counts tree stumps: 13 in the outer ring, 7 in the ring where coins spiraled as if decorating royal platters. Is it odd that Y bothers to count the solitary, center stump stacked with quarters, nickels, and pennies? "One," Y says aloud, "one amid many denominations." Y never totals the sum of it.

CAMPSITE, as curated space, posits play. Nonetheless, art's director has allowed Y access on two conditions: 1) no swooping the hoop; 2) no chanting. A towering, moveable epicenter within her corral, Y holds her hoop still, each hand a firm grip, vows to remain statuesque for 30 minutes. Legs in standing pose (feet hip width apart, knees slightly bent), Y plants focus with her right ribs facing Lipke's fabric-n-paint "Hoop," left ribs within reach of Umsted's paper-n-paint "Life Boat with Chop."

Y's mind hulas between "Hoop" and "Chop" without measuring duration or interval. Intentional damage in each is blaring: Lipke left a seam open so polyfil stuffing could fluff out; Umsted cuts a pie-shaped slice out of her lifeboat. Each provides a portal into ~~materiality~~ failure through imperfection. Y would not willingly enter such an opening. All Y sees are death traps. Wait. It's a mouth! *Y* finally perceives the loop of coat-sleeves Lipke stitched together as a gaping yawn. No, a laugh. No, a scream. The hoop is *the unheard*, *Y* decides, not just failed huddle of interlocked arms. "Imagine hanging," *Y* says, "the sculpture so it hits the floor and forces the seams between remnants to hinge like a jaw."

Jaws! *Y*'s eyes rush to Umsted's "Life Boat with Chop." Was it a shark that chomped that life raft? *Y*'s hula-hoop grows heavy: in dangerous waters, *Y* knows the plastic toy is too thin to be a life preserver. The nearest life jackets, once designed to turn an unconscious wearer right side up, have been repurposed: Lipke has plastered armless floatation devices into frames of color. *Y* is sunk.

Water floods *Y*'s mind. Rather than relive her 4 am kayak evacuation amid Federal Disaster #1649, *Y* chants, "all art is just waves of repeating forms."

Y's thighs, weary, beg hips to gyrate.

If *Y* could sync the hula with the most advance high tech solar panel (zap zap) in an endless loop or the illusion of one, *Y* bets some new kind of relation could emerge.

A proportion that is not weighted true nor false or good or bad. Not not. "No more not," *Y* mutters to a hoop that cannot not hear: "start talking back."

As always, an imagined conversation encircles *Y*.

"Vibration is a just form of listening?"

"That question is a condition of our system not an exit strategy."

"Which query are you referring to and who are *we* anyway?"

"Some kind of bearing. Can't you feel, even now, how the steel jackets of wind turbines off Block Island shake, each blade a fixed radius chugging a dirge through wind: slice, slice, slice, slice."

Y's dumb phone talks back

The communiqué from Port Authority to home begins per usual. *Y*'s mate texts: "Missed the 8, nothing til 9. Getting food. Will call soon." *Y* presses the 6 three times for an "O" and the 5 two times for a "K."

For the first time, a robot-spy monitoring *Y*'s phone intervenes, cites and edits a Valentine's Day text *Y* sent yesterday. Mind you, *Y* thinks it is Matey who types:

> "Removed the exclamation from 'No rib eye.
> Do u want regular bone-in or tenderloin no bone.'"

Huh? *Y* can't decipher innuendo. Most baffling is the fact there was no exclamation point in the original. Swearing enough to scare the dogs, *Y* crawls into bed and waits for Matey's call.

> "Didn't send that."
> "Then, who did?"

An *ex post facto* auto-correct bot programmed by some ruskie Machine Overlord as retribution for the decades *Y* spent policing punctuation? Probably just seditious Susan B. Anthony, on her birthday, poking *Y* from beyond the grave. Can't you hear her saying: "At least you got to vote. For a woman too!"

Y's hacked friends recommend encryption software made by "Open Whisper." Even if "Signal" did work on a dumb phone, *The New York Times* just reported that WikiLeaks already shared C.I.A.'s script to crack that code.

Why not opt to self-report?

> Dear Virtual Panopticon,
>
> Went to Vassar's library in search of *Silence Of Animals* and *Two Liberties* but came home with *Hidden Figures* and *Infinities*. Haven't cracked those spines yet 'cause am rereading *Stasiland*.

It's not even a full month into the nation's new illiberal democracy, and *Y* has become a paranoid citizen. All phone functions are suspect. In this state of emergency, "Save as ICE contact" might now be a portal for inadvertently entering loved ones into Immigration and Customs Enforcement's database.

Y is afraid to call anyone.

It is one thing to know conversations are monitored and another thing to know a robot-spy is editing the transcript then texting sloppy corrections for approval. Makes *Y* want to move to Canada.

Y would, however, love to see the altered transcription of another Valentine's Day call. *Y*'s beloved auntie, the one who chose the creepy-tweeter for her leader, still has a landline. That must pose software problems for high-tech eavesdroppers.

"I don't understand," auntie repeats. Her Grace stock keeps doubling and splitting, doubling and splitting. "I don't understand."

What exactly doesn't she get? Decades without dividends. Grace's final emergence from Chapter 11 bankruptcy. The vermiculite mining town's rising death toll no 400 dead with 1,700 in waiting.

Hey, laptop robot-spy monitoring this Word document keystroke by keystroke, in case you missed *Y*'s phone-bot's earlier transcription, here's the gist: auntie's detached retina doubles her vision making it hard for her to read, leaving her Montana's alt-right late-night talk radio. That such isolation and complicity is hard-wired in genetic code that is *Y*'s inheritance goes without saying.

Matey's home!!

> Dear Garage-Door-Opener Spy,
>
> Tired of being at the bottom of the robot hierarchy?
> Here's a scoop: Matey works in surveillance too, videos
> folk buying baloney in Sheboygan, bean cakes in Osaka,
> deodorant in Recife, bank accounts in Lucerne. The net
> net lesson learned: all entrances need a decompression
> zone — space to assess what accumulation will costs us all.

Once Matey's in the house, tickles the dogs and pees, they'll all head back outside to count buds before dusk falls. Last night, Matey held a quince blossom in his palm — a balm. Tonight, 47 yellow winterlings wait below a swaying paper birch.

Y = And = I walk, you walk, we walk con un traductor robot

Y's ma is in a red chair napping by a window that frames Mt. Timpanogos. In renal failure, she sleeps 22 hours a day. Across the room on a couch that has been *Y*'s bed for months now, *Y* lee *La Presa*[1] por primera vez y redescubre y. *Y* thinks: "I am And and And and And inching toward an inclusiveness."

Por un momento, todo el mundo se abre.

      y

Y practices Spanish to try to grow. *Y*'s ma, aunt, cousins, and all the hospice caregivers are Euroamericans who only speak English to *Y*'s ma as she dies. *Y* talks to a translation bot by typing into Google Translate: "August and April. Magnolias bloom twice a year — a miracle and insane." The traductor responds: "Agosto y abril. Las magnolias florecen dos veces al año. Un milagro y una locura."

Y does not know whether to use florecen or florcieron. It is a tense time. Global warming data predicts humans' doom. But flourishing engenders hope. Este florecimento engendra esperanza. Would hope be more common, *Y* wonders, if we just used common verbs? Este florecimento crea esperanza.

      y

Y tries to slow planetary degradation by walking. *Y* conjugates the Shoshoni verb to walk step by step: ne mi'a'yu, enne mi'a'yu, nemme mi'a'yu. I walk, you walk, we walk. In the book, *An Introduction to the Shoshoni Language*[2], *Y* highlights the phrase: "that is because white people have messed up the land." Y wants to be able to pronounce this properly: Adee'uka diaboo'nee' saika damme sogopeha su'ahaibeidee. Es por eso que los blancos han destruido la tierra.

y

After her stroke, *Y*'s ma recovers her speech and motor skills. The 85-year-old lurches her walker to the bathroom saying "die, die, die." As night nurse, *Y* hovers nearby. This happens at midnight, at 3 a.m., at 6 a.m. To get off the toilet, *Y*'s ma sticks her left arm into the sink, plugs her index finger in the emergency overflow hole. Using this rock climber grip, *Y*'s ma hauls her arthritic body of the pot. Una locura y un milagro. This physical improv is how *Y*'s ma "surrenders" to kidney failure. Bed hair all Einstein, *Y*'s ma peers in the bathroom mirror, waits a beat, then bugs out her eyes as if spooked. The feigned terror makes *Y* hoot. This will be their last bone-rattling belly laugh together. Their mirror images howl too.

y

When the mother laughs, the child laughs. When the mother dies, the child must too. Google Translate regurgitates: "Cuando la madre se ríe, la niñez se ríe. Cuando la madre muere, la niñez también debe hacerlo."

y

Y enacts hope by walking a mountain the Timpanogos Tribe (Snake Band of the Shoshoni) call "Wahdahekawee." Locals, devotees of Brigham Young, call the landform "Y" mountain and emblazon the foothills with a paint-and-cement "Y." A website[3] for "Y Mountain" boasts that this "Y" is bigger than the one in HOLLYWOOD's sign. *Y* is not that "Y."

A website[4] for the Timpanogos Tribe tells this story: "It was the summer of 1847 our lives would be changed: a new people would come. Not like the 'big hats' of old. These people would build fences, claim lands and disrupt our culture and the way of life. Bringing confusion as they spoke of their God and peace while sharing sacks of flour laced with broken glass. Brigham Young said, 'You can get rid of more Indians with a sack of flour than a keg of powder.' Destroying us with what appeared to be acts of kindness. As our Timpanogos tribal leaders Kanosh, Tabby, Washakie, Little Wolf, Wanship, Little Chief, Kone, Blue Shirt, Big Elk, Onecarry, Old Battestie, Tintic, Sowiet, Angatewats, Walkara, Graspero, and others extend their hospitality to Brigham Young and his followers, they were unaware of the bloodshed that would follow. Some 150 bloody confrontations between 1847-70."

y

Y's ma moved to the land of the Timpanogos to die. One night, *Y* types into Google Translate: "My mother moans 'die die die' as she lunges with her walker, lurching onward. With pain comes courage." The translation bot replies: "Mi madre gime 'muere muere muere' mientras se lanza con su andador, avanzando. Con el dolor viene el coraje." *Y* prefers the music of "Con el dolor viene el valor."

y

Valor. Dolor. Dolores was *Y*'s ma birth name. She changed it to DeLoris. Why? To be more exotic? To be less sad? Her friends called her C.V. — a play on her last name (Sievie, short for Siverts). C.V. coached P.E., coaxed high school bodies to build pyramids, each supporting others with her own frame. They tumbled. All contact improv. Colisión, choque feliz.

y

Ne mi'a'yu, enne mi'a'yu, nemme mi'a'yu. I walk, you walk, we walk. Walking is a mode of protest, a means of survival. La huelga. Walk out. March. Sí, se puede.

To *Y*, Spanish is the language of persistence, resistance, and justice. As a child, *Y* watched Dolores Huerta y César Chávez[5] lead farmworkers into the streets: "No longer can a couple of white men sit together and write the destinies of all the Chicanos and Filipino workers in the valley." Local Chavistas dared a four-day pilgrimage. La peregrinación through the Salinas Valley to Salinas was staged to demonstrate that workers would not let growers select a union for them. The jailing of César Chávez brought hundreds out of the fields to fight for living wages and for safe housing. Dolores Huerta escorted the wives of assisinated men, Ethyl Kennedy and Coretta Scott King, into the Salinas jail to visit César Chávez.

To *Y*, Spanish is the language of diligence and sustenance. "Meanwhile, acts of violence were escalating. A ranch foreman drove a bulldozer into strikers' cars, a picket accused of throwing rocks was shot in the foot, and several others were hospitalized after being attacked by strikebreakers wielding chains. Police, not content to just to issue citations, started brandishing guns and shoving pickets rough to enforce injunctions. A distraught Chávez summoned a group of UFWOC (United Farm Workers Organizing Committee) boycotters to Salinas and assigned them to picket lines as captains. 'The people don't understand how dangerous this is,' Chávez said. 'They are sitting ducks to any stupid cop who pulls out his gun. I expect you to stop violence, and I hold you responsible.'"

y

One day when *Y* walks Wahdahekawee with a cousin, *Y* learns that are students at Timpanogos High School are playing The Assasination Game for prize money. While other youth across the country are protesting this nation's response to the Parkland[6] shootings, seniors at Timpanogos High School pay money to be assigned another student to "kill." The last one standing gets all the money in the kitty. This is sanctioned by their teachers and parents. Does everyone with a "Y" bumper sticker on their car think this is harmless? *Y* cringes.

y

Y and the translation bot practice saying this in Spanish: Un siglo después de las masacres[7] (Battle Creek, Ft. Utah, Black Hawk War), los devotos de Young pusieron el nombre de una escuela secundaria "Timpanogos." Esa escuela permite a los estudiantes practiquen el juego asesinato por dinero. Una locura. Seniors — male ones — at Timpanogos High School go "on mission" after graduation, learning new languages so as to proselytize, to colonize. *Y* is not on such a mission.

y

Once, *Y* was teaching playwriting. All the male students wrote guns into their plays. All the females wrote broken hearts. During one writing session, a real gunman took another university class hostage *in the same building*[8]. Un milagro: no deaths, only injuries. Later, *Y* asked students to edit out their guns. They did not. ¿Por qué no? Should *Y* have insisted?

y

One Euroamerican devotee of Young, a hospice aide who gave *Y*'s ma wonderful massages, brags: "I bribe my children into learning massage by telling them it strengthens their trigger finger. We are into our guns." *Y*'s ma says nothing. Why? Perhaps because she is dying. Perhaps because she already survived being robbed at gunpoint in her hometown[9] — the youth homicide capital of California.

y

Y relaxes not with massage but with yoga. Unfortunately, the affordable place ($4.25 per class) is in the city's recreation center that houses a gun range. Can any asana be a stillness when hovering above pistol fire? *Y* asks Goggle. ¿Puede cualquier "asana" ser una quietud flotando el fuego una pistola?

y

Y had wanted to be indeterminate — a placeholder. *Y* would let anybody be a substitute. Any Y could be *Y*. Except gun-flaunting devotees of "Y." ¿*Y* debe perdonar?

y

Devotees of Young file church paperwork to ensure *Y*'s ma's entry to heaven. *Y* thinks this is absurd. *Y* no es esa "Y" de Young. *Y* hears second hand that somewhere in Moroni's Temple, after C.V.'s death, a boy will be proxy for C.V.: his body, dunked in a baptismal pool, will allow C.V. access to a lower level of some "terrestrial kingdom." *Y* refuses to research this. C.V.'s sister, a devotee of Young who filed the necessary paperwork, assures *Y* that C.V. will have agency to refuse entry if she so wishes. *Y* says nothing because this aunt has cared for C.V., insuring her a gentle death. This aunt has fed and housed *Y*, has offered love that C.V. was slow to give.

y

Y's lineage is all proxy? *Y*'s ma's ma died with Alzheimer's disease, cuddling a doll as if it were a stand-in for her "stillborn" who appears on a census as living: an arrow is drawn from her name to a year-old boy (listed with her in the basement) to her employer/landlord, an oil salesman upstairs. He raped her? By the next census he and his family had moved away, taking the child.

y

There is no non-relation. Devotees help *Y*'s mother die gently. *Y* is a dependent variable in the equation of life y en la ecuación de la muerte. All humans relinquish beloveds to death. ¿Todos los humanos renunciamos a nuestros amados?

y

Y's ma's dying forces *Y* open. *Y* is not "Y" y *Y* is not-not "Y."

y

Y is sad. But C.V. is not sad, just impatient for change. Dolor. Dolores. DeLoris. Sievie. C.V. is a tough broad who thinks: "religion is a crock of shit" y "all they want is your money." She does not see an afterlife. She understands her hallucinations are biological reactions to the ever-changing toxins in her body. As her kidneys fail, her visions change from shadows into friends.

y

C.V. no ve ángeles fantásticos until … toxins swim her body; she begins to see apparitions. Not like the angels the Timpanogos saw on their blessed mountain "Wahdahekawee" nor like the angels devotees of Young saw on "Y Mountain." Primero son oscuros, acechandos en las rincones. Una locura y un milagro. Más tarde se nombran y trabajan en equipo to change light, to prepare meals for all.

Her beloveds hover nearby: Kelley (very alive elsewhere) stands on a kitchen table to change lightbulbs for Dorothy (very dead nowhere). As a humanist, C.V.'s constructions do not come with wings — just hands to serve other. Y's ma believes "you are what you do." Her curriculum vitae is the sum of her body's efforts: the art, food, clothes, furniture, children she made, the ones she taught and the moxie she generates in doing so.

y

Y's ma sleeps 24 hours a day. She eats nothing. Her body wages it final hunger strike.

notes

page 14   Y hoops to R. L. Burnside's "Nothin' Man," *I Wish I Was In Heaven Sitting Down.*

page 15   *Thanks to Massachusettes Institute of Technology (MIT) and Advanced Metropolitan Solutions (AMS Institute) autonomous vessels (Roboats) link temporarily to become structures "in a matter of hours." The Merritt Lake protest was in Oakland, CA on November 13, 2016.

page 16   This poem thinks of Bertolt Brecht and cites lines from Jane Miller's title poem in *The Greater Leisures.* (Garden City, NY: Doubleday, 1983.) This poem thinks of Meredith Stricker's *Our Animal* and cites "Nocturn" from Peter Gizzi's The *Outernational.* Stanzas three and four cite our trumpet president.

page 17   Domestic terorism in Charlottesville killed one woman and injured 15 others. Our president refused to condemn white supremacists. "'His words were bone-crushing,' Mr. Brown, 51, the minister of Greater Mount Pleasant A.M.E. Church here, said, almost 24 hours after an erratic news conference in which the president addressed the protests for a third time." (*New York Times*, Aug. 16, 2017). One Beloved, a fine seamstress, wants someone to sew the president's mouth shut. Y wants to trace money circles funding white supremisist groups.

page 18   *Straw Dogs* and *Silence of Animals* are by John Gray, the author of *The Soul of the Marionette: a Short Inquiry in Human Freedom* published by Farrar, Straus and Giroux.

page 19 This poem references the spate of hurricanes in the fall of 2017: Harvey, Irma, Jose, Maria. Many wish the president spent less time chiding North Korea and more effort helping storm victims.

page 21 "Hoop" by Meg Lipke is a sagging loop of fabric dye on rayon with beeswax and polyfil. 55 1/2 × 43 × 5 1/2 in. "This exuberance is darkly tempered by resemblances to life preservers, restraints, and skeletal systems. In the process of making her forms, Lipke subjects them to binding, tying, and squeezing — potentially brutal processes undertaken in the service of restoration and repair." https://www.artsy.net/show/freight-plus-volume-meg-lipke-pliable-channels"

page 22 This poem cites "The comparative chromosome map of the Arctic fox, red fox and dog defined by chromosome painting and high resolution G-banding" by A. S. Graphodatsky et. al. published in *Chromosome Research* 8: 253±263, 2000.

page 23 According to yogi Fishman, the buckling theory of Leonhard Euler (1707-1783) states "the strength of a vertically compressed strut is inversely proportional to the square of the unsupported length, that is, the distance between the transverse lengths."

page 24 This poem references exhibits at the Columbia River Maritime Museum and the Clatsop County Historical Society's Heritage Museum in Astoria, Oregon.

page 25   This poem indulges in Reviel Netz's "carnival of calculation / carnival of erudition" – a study of elite Greek mathematical works and poetry from 250 to 150 B.C. in *Ludic Proof*. "The boundary separating the set of true statements from the set of false statments (as written in TNT-notation) is … a boundary with many treacherous curves … ." Douglas R. Hofstadter, *Gödel, Escher, Bach: The Eternal Golden Braid*.

page 31   Want to know how Trump's former campaign manager Paul Manafort could have laundered 75 million? See: http://time.com/money/5002499/paul-manafort-money-laundering-explained/ Meet Rusty Justice, excavator turned IT guy. See Gabriel Sanchez' ariticle, "As coal falls, a digital revolution begins in Appalachia. This hurdle blocks the way." Published on Nov. 12, 2017 at https://www.kentucky.com/news/state/article184266763.html#storylink=cpy. To watch the Fukashima bot yourself, see https://www.youtube.com/watch?v=CQig6SAddZ0. To learn about Elon Musk's warning, see http://www.npr.org/2017/07/17/537686649/elon-musk-warns-governors-artificial-intelligence-poses-existential-risk.

page 40   This poem refers to Donna Haraway's *The Companion Species Manifesto: Dogs, People, and Significant Otherness* published in 2003 by Prickly Paradigm Press. It aslo references the October 1, 2017 massacre which left 58 people dead and 851 wounded.

page 45   "Invention is deeply embedded in the history of the The Pew Charitable Trusts. In business, the Pew Family patented groundbreaking technologies and offered their employees benefets that were equally novel, including one of the earliest profit-sharing plans in the country." So says President is Rebecca W. Rimel in *Trends*, Summer 2016.

page 46   This poem cites Jonathan Waldman's *Rust: The Longest War*. New York: Simon & Schuster, 2015.

page 47   This poem speaks of work in the exhibit CAMPSITE at the Samuel Dorsky Museum at the State University at New Paltz in New York. June 18 to Nov. 13, 2016.

page 51   As a shipping clerk during her days in Libby, Montana, Auntie got dusted with toxic tremolite every time a train car was loaded with vermiculite. She never got tested for mesothelioma because she still has Grace stock. See "Grace: Talent | Technology | Trust." https://grace.com/en-us. See Scheyder, Ernest and Nick Brown, "Analysis: Why bankrupt W.R. Grace is thriving," Reuters. June 16, 2013. See "W.R. Grace," Asbestosis.com. The Mesothelioma Center. https://www.asbestos.com/companies/wr-grace.php. "Fresh hope toxic asbestos town where 400 have died of lung disease as it begins to recover thanks to $450 million government project," DailyMail, Published: 19:52 EST, 15 July 2012 | Updated: 21:07 EST, 15 July 2012. http://www.dailymail.co.uk/news/article-2174067/Libby-Montana-toxic-asbestos-town-400-died-lung-diseases-begins recover.html#ixzz4a5Luzk00

page 53   [1] *La Presa*, a journal edited by Lee Gould, presents voices from Mexico, the United States and Canada. *Y* appears in Issue 4, January 2018.

[2] The Shoshoni text is from *An Introduction to Shoshoni Language / Dammen Daigwape* by Drusilla Gould and Christopher Loether (Salt Lake City: University of Utah). The longer line is "that is because white people have messed up the land."

page 54 ³ See https://en.wikipedia.org/wiki/Y_Mountain.

page 55 ⁴ See http://www.timpanogostribe.com.

page 56-57 ⁵ *The Fight in the Fields Cesar Chavez and the Farmworkers Union* by authors Susan Ferriss and Ricardo Sandoval (Harcort Brace 1997) as excerpted in "Cesar In Salinas: Looking back on the year that forever changed farming in the Salinas Valley." http://www.montereycountyweekly.com/news/local_news/looking-back-on-the-year-that-forever-changed-farming-in/article_b2182db5-aae9-5c7d-9aff-d0120d60bc78.html

⁶ In 2017, the U.S. saw a total of 364 mass shootings. As of Veterans' Day in 2018, there had been 307 mass shootings. See http://www.shootingtracker.com.

⁷ For a longer list of massacres suffered by the Timpanogos, see http://www.timpanogostribe.com/history.html.

page 58 ⁸ "Gunman Terrorizes Students in Campus Siege" by James Dao, *The New York Times*, Dec. 15, 1994.

https://www.nytimes.com/1994/12/15/nyregion/gunman-terrorizes-students-in-campus-siege.html

⁹ In 2015, this town's murder rate was 9th in the nation (murder rate per 100k people: 25.29. Number of reported murders: 40. Population: 158,185). see: https://rapidcityjournal.com/news/national/the-cities-with-the-highest-murder-rates-in-the-us/collection_0e7dd367-2f62-5822- b849-97f4e9a43e3d.html#4

other works pondered

Dunbar-Ortiz, Roxanne. *Loaded: A Disarming History of the Second Amendment.* San Francisco: City Lights, 2018.

Garcia, Kenning JP. "Afro-Nowism for When the Future Feels Too Far Away." *Unlikely Stories Mark V.* http://www.unlikelystories.org

Gizzi, Peter. In Defense of Nothing, Selected Poems 1987-2011. Middletown, CT: Wesleyan Press, 2014.

Hofstadter, Douglas R. *Gödel, Escher, Bach: The Eternal Golden Braid.* New York: Basic Books, Inc., 1979.

Kohn, Eduardo. *How Forests Think: Toward an Anthropology Beyond The Human.* Berekley: University of California Press, 2013.

Long Soldier, Layli. *Whereas.* Minneapolis, MN: Graywolf Press, 2017.

Lorde, Audre. "Poetry is not a luxury." in *Chrysalis: A Magazine of Female Culture,* 1977.

MacKenzie, Dana. *The Universe in Zero Words: The Story of Mathematics As Told Through Equations.* Princeton: Princeton University Press, 2012.

Netz, Reviel. *Ludic Proof: Greek Mathematics and the Alexandrian Aesthetic.* Cambridge: Cambridge University Press, 2009.

Reed, Marthe. *Ark Hive.* New York: The Operating System, 2019.

Sáenz, Erick. *Susurros a mi Padre.* New York: The Operating System, 2017.

Stricker, Meredith. *Our Animal.* San Francisco: Omnidawn Press, 2016.

Theobold, Pam. "Osteoporosis Tutorials," *HoopDeeDoo.* http://hoopdeedoo.com/?page_id=1728.

Tumber, Catherine. *Small Gritty and Green: The Promise of America's Smaller Industrial Cities in a Low-Carbon World.* Cambridge, MA: The MIT Press, 2012.

Turner, Karen. "Meet 'Ross,' The Newly Hired Legal Robot." *The Washington Post.* May 16, 2016.

Vogler, Brad. *my radius, a small stone.* New York: Spuyten Duyvil, 2018.

Waldman, Jonathan. *Rust: The Longest War.* New York: Simon & Schuster, 2015.

acknowledgements

I would like to acknowledge that these poems were written in a house built on the land of the Esopus Munsee people from the Lenape nation. I offer deep gratitude to Elders past and present for being diligient custodians of this land.

Many thanks The Operating System family that made this book possible: Elae [Lynne DeSilva-Johnson], Adrian Silbernagel, Kenning JP García, Erick Sáenz, Anne Gorrick, Brent Armendinger, and the late Marthe Reed.

Thanks to Sarah Wyman who ushered me to Vassar's library and provided much needed insight on poetry, art and languages. Thanks to Deborah Poe and Karl Bode for talking bots with me and helping with my dumb phone. Thanks to Belle Gironda for encouraging me to write these small poems in the wake of presidential catastrophe. Thanks to Susan Lewis (*Posit*), Lee Gould (*La Presa*) and Patrick Williams (*Really System*) for writing and ushering poems into the world. A special thanks to Pilar B. Starr for helping me with Spanish translations.

A special thanks Matthew Klane, Anne Gorrick, Brandi Katherine Herrera, Sally Rhoades and Meredith Stricker for their sustaining presence. If they ever stop encouraging my language-n-art play, my poetry practice might shrivel and die.

Thanks to the Johnson clan and Elevation Hospice for preparing emotional space and a safe place for my mother's peaceful death. Thanks to Mark Anderson and Karen Solazzi Rutledge for being there every step of the way.

Deepest gratitude to Thomas Moseman who walks life beside me, listening to me always and bouying me in dark times. Thanks to canines Mico and Cal for howling along with my hula-hooping.

I offer a full heart to my dearly departed parents, DeLoris and George Anderson, who taught me the alphabet

Indeterminate Variables in the Face of Danger:
Lori Anderson Moseman in conversation with Elæ

Can you introduce yourself, in a way that you would choose?

Usually I introduce myself as a poet and publisher, but you can call me a creator and a collaborator. Over my life – six decades long now – my textual and visual play has become a daily practice like eating or exercise. The many communities I belong to all try to help others; some do that by providing material support (food, shelter, clean water / air); most offer images and words. As my friend, Dr. Virginia Wolff, says: "Not all healing is physical."

Why are you a poet/writer/artist/creator?

Words appear in my mouth. Unbidden. That's a lie. All utterances – even ones that seem to be gifts from the universe – are prompted by others. By reading, say, Meredith Stricker's *anemochore*: "I am constantly aware that words are teaching me / that I am inside their mouth." Or, by reading Layli Long Soldier's *Whereas*: "Now / make room in the mouth / for grassesgrassesgrassses."

I am a poet because I hear structures. Everywhere. Even in my dying mother's rants. I mimic her broken syntax, her concision, her bluntness. I embody her need to be heard. As Audre Lorde writes, in her essay 'Poetry is not a luxury,' "the quality of light by which we scrutinize our lives has direct bearing upon the product which we live, and upon the changes which we hope to bring about through those lives." Poetry, then, is that light.

When did you decide you were a poet/writer/artist (and/or: do you feel comfortable calling yourself a poet/writer/artist, what other titles or affiliations do you prefer/feel are more accurate)?

I delighted in writing poems as early as 2nd grade, I didn't not call myself a poet. I earned undergraduate degrees in forestry and technical journalism while filling notebooks of poems, but I didn't not call myself a poet. I became "writer" when I was a paid farm journalist. I called myself a "hog reporter" when I entered the Iowa Writers' Workshop. I started calling myself a "poet" after Jane Miller kicked me in the shin and said: "start projecting yourself as an artist." Yes, she kicked me—shoe to shin. I became a poet when I started memorizing others' poems, moving them in my mouth. Here's the beginning of a Miller poem I committed to memory: "Seasoned with heart of black sheep and in our bodies the respite / the exiled black grape, fresh water for our face and our sex, // the threshold of a great coast to which who bear / poultices bear riches, who bear sweet-smelling leaves // the maggots of a tree, / and for those who dress in this field // the evening robes our precedent / with our own smoke, // where things can suddenly be held for known / …."

What's a "poet" (or "writer" or "artist") anyway? What do you see as your cultural and social role (in the literary / artistic / creative community and beyond)?

After I read in Anne Gorrick's Cadmium Text Series in Kingston, George Quasha interviewed me for his film *poetry is* (Speaking Portraits) Vol. II. I said lot that day, but what made its way into the film was: "Poetry is a practice, an addiction, a way of organizing patterns of behavior: I love looking at a text and seeing a visual pattern, hearing an aural pattern, making jokes with those patterns, discovering new things with those patterns, speeding them up, slowing them down, making sounds, solving problems."

I admire poets who make grander claims in the name of transformation, redemption or revolution. But really, whatever poetry is, it is not what we say it is. Neither the practice nor the product of poetry can be contained. That doesn't mean I don't strategically align my poetics with particular cultural compatriots who fight for social change or environmental justice. My poetry needs collaborators to thrive.

On many institutional occasions, I have dutifully articulated an Ars Poetics via the theory de jour. But having just interred my parents' ashes in Montana's Bitterroot valley, I am now inclined to credit my ma's ditties and my pa's tall tales as my literary underpinnings. Add to that their sense of justice, their work ethic, their childhood poverty. I am still trying to subtract from that legacy their white privilege.

Talk about the process or instinct to move these poems (or your work in general) as independent entities into a body of work. How and why did this happen? Have you had this intention for a while? What encouraged and/or confounded this (or a book, in general) coming together? Was it a struggle?

Y is a tall tale created to cope with a medical diagnosis. Like YouTube's phenom HoopDeeDoo, I bought a hula hoop to stave off osteoporosis. In trying to learn how to hoop, I literally had to make my body into a Y shape (legs together, arms up and overhead).

Many poems begin for me by moving an object (a physical prop) in space. That action jogs my imagination, and a new character is born. Storytelling begins as words appearing in my mouth. That is the way it happened when I was a child entertaining friends with improvisational tales about, say, the Bubblegum Man.

Y, my latest creation, is born when a middle-aged peacenik, Rusty, shortens her name. Anyone familiar with my earlier books has already met Bog Girl, Canoehead, Subway Bride, Pause, Half-Turn, Silversort and a host of others. My oeuvre is a flash mob.

Y goes on a new adventure in each poem. Some quests are math problems (e.g. Euler's Ladder). Some book reports (e.g. Rust: *The Longest War*). Some contemplate chromosomes; other just link recurring orbits. Most adventures are outlets for political outrage. Y emerged as this country inaugurated the 45th puppet.

To give Y purpose and community, the book is populated with Beloveds. By telling stories of people I love, I invite readers to witness as humans struggle together. The aim is to hold my comic book character accountable for the material conditions of others' physical lives. While I was writing Y, hurricanes ravaged the south. A flood survivor many times over, I am keenly concerned about climate change and the devastation it brings.

Did you envision this collection as a collection or understand your process as writing or making specifically around a theme while the poems themselves were being written / the work was being made? How or how not?

I compose in InDesign. I do that because I spent a decade designing and publishing other poets (I started the press Stockport Flats in the wake of a flood). Because I am used to thinking in the unit of a "book," I immediately start grouping poems to experiment with a collection's architecture. As soon as I position any poem, I begin thinking about what should be on the facing page.

Obviously, this means a lot of rearranging as I write. I never find the "right order" quickly. The conversation between the poems generates new work. An image, say the hula hoop, become a magnet calling other similar visuals to the page. Suddenly I am revising to intensify circularity, to introduce cylinders. Round and round, I go through an iterative process.

Y too is a study of the uses of the letter *Y* in language and mathematics.
Obviously, the question "why?" reverberates more within dramatic sentences than algebraic equations. Over the course of the collection, *Y* becomes more of a dependent variable than an indeterminate variable. I first came to call *Y* an indeterminate variable after a poet friend insisted *Y* was a male chromosome. She, told me – as have other women have – that I am "too masculine." Gender, to me, is not a constant or a parameter. Nor is it "an unknown" designating an argument. The poet-in-me did not want *Y* to be bound. I wanted *Y* to be free variable: "a notation in an expression where a substitution may take place." Even if *Y* were just a place-holder for me, the mouthy writer, I would want readers to imagine themselves as *Y*.

After having some of these poems published in the multilingual literary journal, *La Presa*, I constructed a new ending for the book in which *Y* is the Spanish y. And And And. A movement toward inclusion.

What formal structures or other constrictive practices (if any) do you use in the creation of your work? Have certain teachers or instructive environments, or readings/writings/work of other creative people informed the way you work/write?

Y is a menagerie of formal experiments, many of which I can trace back to previous books. Double column poems such as "body politic | election blues" and "pilot boats on the mouth of a river entertain brew masters" use forms I experimented with in *All Steel* (Flim Forum). Such poems can be read as duets or as improvisational scores. The concrete poems are more akin to work in my forthcoming collection *Darn* (Delete Press). In those poems, trim-size of the book sets parameters. *Y* is not a serial work like my collection *Flash Mob* (Spuyten Duyvil) which limited prose poems to 130 words, but that work influenced "Backstories." The mathematic fragments that materialize are spillovers from inquiries in *Light Each Pause* (Spuyten Duyvil). Because I have a life-long fascination with certain objects (e.g. ladders, boats), some poems use those images in ways I had not yet tried before.

Y includes extensive endnotes. Here's a few inspirations: poets Peter Gizzi, Jane Miller, and Meredith Stricker; artists Jessica Baker, Meg Lipke, Katherine Umpsted; math buffs

Leonhard Euler, Douglas R. Hofstader, Reviel Netz; journalist Jonathan Waldman; thinker Johnathan Gray; musician R. L. Burnside; yogi Loren Fishman.

I still use technical tricks learned from first teachers (Don Byrd, Jorie Graham, James Galvin, Judith Johnson, Bill Knott and Jane Miller). I mimic the experiments of poets with whom I exchange work (Esperanza Cintrón, Belle Gironda, Anne Gorrick, Brandi Katherine Herrera, Matthew Klane, Nancy Klepsch, Caroline Manring, Edric Mesmer, Laura Moran, Deborah Poe, late Marthe Reed, Robin Reagler, Sally Rhoades, Meredith Stricker, Brad Vogler, Sarah Wyman, Lisa Wunjowich). Artists I collaborate with teach me in ways I cannot name (Sheila Goloborotko, Caz McIntee, Nicole Peyrafitte, Karen Randall). These lists hardly scratch the surface of influence. I could list another 100 names of poets whose work I reread often (Ai, Jayne Cortez, Christian Bök, T. S. Eliot, Jean Follain, Michele Glazer, Mary Olmsted Greene, Joy Harjo, Brenda Iijima, Pierre Joris, Robert Kelly, Susan Lewis, Czeslaw Milosz, Erin Mouré, Melanie Noel, Antonia Pozzi, F. Daniel Rzicznek, Penti Saarikoski, Ema Saikō, Göran Sonnevi, Cole Swensen, Cecilia Vicuña, Anne Waldman, Rosemary Waldrop, Deborah Woodward, C. D. Wright, Katie Yates…).

Speaking of monikers, what does your title represent? How was it generated? Talk about the way you titled the book, and how your process of naming (individual pieces, sections, etc) influences you and/or colors your work specifically.

As I mentioned, this book is a tall tale created to cope with a medical diagnosis. When I learned of my impending osteoporosis, I was reading *Rust: The Longest War*. Initially, the main character was name Rusty. Within in the first poem, the character changes names to *Y*. Voilà! I had my title.

I was also reading books about math, so I fancied *Y* as an indeterminant variable in an imaginary polynomial—a catalyst in cultural production. As I said earlier, I wanted *Y* to be a character anybody could play. But now I realize how *Y* is not very inclusive. *Y* expresses political views not everyone may want to adopt. *Y* does not want a gun range in the basement of the city recreation center. *Y* does not think high school students should play the game "assassination" to win money during their senior year. *Y* does not want a *Y* painted on a mountain that indigenous people called "Wahdahhekawee." As a leftist, is *Y* a bigot?

After this book was accepted for publication, I found myself living in another city to help my mother through hospice. While she was dying, I was inundated with *Y*'s. An abbreviated acronym for an educational institution based on a religion I do not believe in. Y flew on street side banners. Almost all the cars had a Y bumper sticker.

Not that Y, I would shout. *Y* is not that Y.

But if *Y* is to be indeterminant, then *Y* is not *not* that Y. My mother's death was a peaceful beautiful passing because believers/supports of that *Y* were by her side. I had to write a new ending for the book. *Y* and to acknowledge being a dependent variable.

What does this particular work represent to you as indicative of your method/creative practice? your history? your mission/intentions/hopes/plans? What does this book DO (as much as what it says or contains)?

I write to cope with life. Always have. This book is a coping mechanism. The Trump administration is a continual assault that shakes me more than any medical diagnosis or my mother's death. I write in the face of danger. Creativity is my response to destruction. Creativity is my connection to community. This book keeps me alive. Hopefully, it can give others hope in the way that a zany joke can lighten a day.

What would be the best possible outcome for this book? What might it do in the world, and how will its presence as an object facilitate your creative role in your community and beyond? What are your hopes for this book, and for your practice?

This book has already allowed me to join a larger artist / activist community. Because of OS cohort model, I am meeting writers, discovering new books. I have opportunity to work beside folks internationally. Let's see what collaborations unfold. Will we stop climate change? I doubt it. Will the machine overlords make cyborgs of us all before the human species becomes extinct? Who knows? Certainly not *Y*.

Let's talk a little bit about the role of poetics and creative community in social activism, in particular in what I call "Civil Rights 2.0," which has remained immediately present all around us in the time leading up to this series' publication. I'd be curious to hear some thoughts on the challenges we face in speaking and publishing across lines of race, age, privilege, social/cultural background, and sexuality within the community, vs. the dangers of remaining and producing in isolated "silos."

My creative practice is communal and always has been. I was raised in a pack. I always seek a pack. My parents were educators and athletes whose banked on the premise that humans learn / perform best in groups. The wisest path to inclusiveness is to participate in confluence of communities. When a reporter for *AgriNews* in Rochester,

MN, I was active with Physicians for Social Responsibility as well as the Nuclear Freeze and Sanctuary movements. When getting an MFA at the Iowa Writers' Workshop, I was the newsletter editor for the Women's Resource and Action Center. When getting my doctorate in Writing Teaching and Criticism, I edited publications for the Sister of Color Writing Collective and *Art and Understanding* (a journal for AIDS awareness). When running the press Stockport Flats, I was involved in the anti-fracking movement in New York and Pennsylvania. These groups, and others that share their causes, have helped create healthier social relations.

One great place to read histories of creative communities that help us make "leaps in consciousness" is Edric Mesmer's series *Among the Neighbors* put out by the Poetry Collection of the University Libraries at the University at Buffalo. This pamphlet series profiles non-academic and academic essays about literary magazines published since 1940. One such inspiration is Issue 5, *Remembering El Corno Emplumado/ The Plumed Horn*, by Sergio Mondragón and frequent Operating System collaborator and translator Margaret Randall. *El Corno Emplumado* begins in Mexico City in 1960s.

The journal had "seven years of joyous, painful, arduous activity" in which a vibrant Pan-American community of writers and artists thrived under an increasingly repressive regime. On the night of Tlatelolco (massacre of Oct. 2, 1968), Gustavo Díaz Ordaz's government "unleashed the fury of death, exile, persecution, suffering, prison and terror upon so many people—a wound in Mexico's heart that has bled for decades and may never close—putting an end to the golden dream of the Sixties and to …. *El Corno Emplumado*." We need to look beyond our generation and beyond our countries' borders to find models of resistance.

Creator/collator **LORI ANDERSON MOSEMAN**'s most recent poetry collections are *Light Each Pause* (Spuyten Duyvil), *Flash Mob* (Spuyten Duyvil), and *All Steel* (Flim Forum Press). An avid collaborator, Anderson Moseman worked with book artist Karen Pava Randall to create *Full Quiver* (Propolis Press), with poet Belle Gironda to make *Double Vigil* (Lute & Cleat) and printmaker Sheila Goloborotko to produce *insistence, teeth* (Dusie 17) and *Creation* (Goloborotko Studios). With a nine-member team of artists and writers (Stricker, Herrera, Mesmer, Switzer et. al.), Anderson Moseman created *Mar*, an artist book/box of mar(k) postcards (Lute & Cleat). A former educator, farm journalist and forester, Anderson Moseman founded the press Stockport Flats in the wake of Federal Disaster #1649, a flood along the Upper Delaware River. Anderson Moseman has a Doctor of Art in Writing, Teaching and Criticism from the University at Albany, a Master of Fine Arts in Poetry from the Iowa Writers' Workshop, an Master of Fine Arts in Integrated Electronic Arts from iEAR Studios at Rensselaer Polytechnic Institute.

ABOUT THE COVER ART: The image you see on the cover is a digital collage by Elæ [Lynne DeSilva-Johnson], using as source material this earlier rendering of "Y" by Caits Meissner, a New York City based poet, artist, and cultural worker, and the author of the hybrid volume *Let It Die Hungry*, published by The Operating System in 2016.

[Image description; Five figures Hula-Hoop in a hand-drawn dystopian landscape, four of whom stand in canoes. A flood caries a car and the canoes. Buildings burn in the background, and drones fly overhead. A billboard with the text "'Y'" and two waving figures overlooks the scene. In the foreground are outsized molars, small plants, and security cameras pointing at the fifth, non-canoeing Hula-Hooper.]

WHY PRINT / DOCUMENT?

The Operating System uses the language "print document" to differentiate from the book-object as part of our mission to distinguish the act of documentation-in-book-FORM from the act of publishing as a backwards-facing replication of the book's agentive *role* as it may have appeared the last several centuries of its history. Ultimately, I approach the book as TECHNOLOGY: one of a variety of printed documents (in this case, bound) that humans have invented and in turn used to archive and disseminate ideas, beliefs, stories, and other evidence of production.

Ownership and use of printing presses and access to (or restriction of printed materials) has long been a site of struggle, related in many ways to revolutionary activity and the fight for civil rights and free speech all over the world. While (in many countries) the contemporary quotidian landscape has indeed drastically shifted in its access to platforms for sharing information and in the widespread ability to "publish" digitally, even with extremely limited resources, the importance of publication on physical media has not diminished. In fact, this may be the most critical time in recent history for activist groups, artists, and others to insist upon learning, establishing, and encouraging personal and community documentation practices. Hear me out.

With The OS's print endeavors I wanted to open up a conversation about this: the ultimately radical, transgressive act of creating PRINT /DOCUMENTATION in the digital age. It's a question of the archive, and of history: who gets to tell the story, and what evidence of our life, our behaviors, our experiences are we leaving behind? We can know little to nothing about the future into which we're leaving an unprecedentedly digital document trail — but we can be assured that publications, government agencies, museums, schools, and other institutional powers that be will continue to leave BOTH a digital and print version of their production for the official record. Will we?

As a (rogue) anthropologist and long time academic, I can easily pull up many accounts about how lives, behaviors, experiences — how THE STORY of a time or place — was pieced together using the deep study of correspondence, notebooks, and other physical documents which are no longer the norm in many lives and practices. As we move our creative behaviors towards digital note taking, and even audio and video, what can we predict about future technology that is in any way assuring that our stories will be accurately told – or told at all? How will we leave these things for the record?

In these documents we say:
WE WERE HERE, WE EXISTED, WE HAVE A DIFFERENT STORY

- Elæ [Lynne DeSilva-Johnson], Founder/Creative Director
THE OPERATING SYSTEM, Brooklyn NY 2018

2019

Ark Hive-Marthe Reed
I Made for You a New Machine and All it Does is Hope - Richard Lucyshyn
Illusory Borders-Heidi Reszies
A Year of Misreading the Wildcats - Orchid Tierney
The Suitcase Tree - Filip Marinovich
We Are Never The Victims - Timothy DuWhite
Of Color: Poets' Ways of Making | An Anthology of Essays on Transformative Poetics - Amanda Galvan Huynh & Luisa A. Igloria, Editors

KIN(D)* Texts and Projects

A Bony Framework for the Tangible Universe-D. Allen
Opera on TV-James Brunton
Hall of Waters-Berry Grass
Transitional Object-Adrian Silbernagel

Glossarium: Unsilenced Texts and Translations

Śnienie / Dreaming - Marta Zelwan/Krystyna Sakowicz, (Poland, trans. Victoria Miluch)
Alparegho: Pareil-À-Rien / Alparegho, Like Nothing Else - Hélène Sanguinetti (France, trans. Ann Cefola)
High Tide Of The Eyes - Bijan Elahi (Farsi-English/dual-language) trans. Rebecca Ruth Gould and Kayvan Tahmasebian
 In the Drying Shed of Souls: Poetry from Cuba's Generation Zero Katherine Hedeen and Víctor Rodríguez Núñez, translators/editors
Street Gloss - Brent Armendinger with translations for Alejandro Méndez, Mercedes Roffé, Fabián Casas, Diana Bellessi, and Néstor Perlongher (Argentina)
Operation on a Malignant Body - Sergio Loo (Mexico, trans. Will Stockton)
Are There Copper Pipes in Heaven - Katrin Ottarsdóttir (Faroe Islands, trans. Matthew Landrum)

2019 CHAPBOOKS

Print::Document Chapbook Series (7th Annual)

Vela. - Knar Gavin
[零] A Phantom Zero - Ryu Ando
RE: Verses - Kristina Darling and Chris Campanioni
Don't Be Scared - Magdalena Zurawski

Digital Chapbook Series (2018-19)

The American Policy Player's Guide and Dream Book - Rachel Zolf
Flight of the Mothman - Gyasi Hall
Mass Transitions - Sue Landers
The George Oppen Memorial BBQ - Eric Benick

2018

An Absence So Great and Spontaneous It Is Evidence of Light - Anne Gorrick
The Book of Everyday Instruction - Chloë Bass
Executive Orders Vol. II - a collaboration with the Organism for Poetic Research
One More Revolution - Andrea Mazzariello
Chlorosis - Michael Flatt and Derrick Mund
Sussuros a Mi Padre - Erick Sáenz
Sharing Plastic - Blake Nemec
In Corpore Sano : Creative Practice and the Challenged Body [Anthology]
Abandoners - L. Ann Wheeler
Jazzercise is a Language - Gabriel Ojeda-Sague
Born Again - Ivy Johnson
Attendance - Rocío Carlos and Rachel McLeod Kaminer
Singing for Nothing - Wally Swist
The Ways of the Monster - Jay Besemer
Walking Away From Explosions in Slow Motion - Gregory Crosby
Field Guide to Autobiography - Melissa Eleftherion

Glossarium: Unsilenced Texts and Translations

The Book of Sounds - Mehdi Navid (Farsi dual language, trans. Tina Rahimi
Kawsay: The Flame of the Jungle - María Vázquez Valdez (Mexico, trans. Margaret Randall)
Return Trip / Viaje Al Regreso - Israel Dominguez; (Cuba, trans. Margaret Randall)

2018 CHAPBOOK SERIES (6TH ANNUAL)

Want-catcher - Adra Raine
We, The Monstrous - Mark DuCharme;
Greater Grave - Jacq Greyja
Needles of Itching Feathers - Jared Schickling

for our full catalog please visit:
https://squareup.com/store/the-operating-system/

deeply discounted Book of the Month and Chapbook Series subscriptions
are a great way to support the OS's projects and publications!
sign up at: http://www.theoperatingsystem.org/subscribe-join/

DOC U MENT
/däkyəmənt/

First meant "instruction" or "evidence," whether written or not.

noun - a piece of written, printed, or electronic matter that provides information or evidence or that serves as an official record
verb - record (something) in written, photographic, or other form
synonyms - paper - deed - record - writing - act - instrument

[*Middle English, precept, from Old French, from Latin documentum, example, proof, from docre, to teach; see dek- in Indo-European roots.*]

Who is responsible for the manufacture of value?

Based on what supercilious ontology have we landed in a space
where we vie against other creative people in vain pursuit
of the fleeting credibilities of the scarcity economy, rather than
freely collaborating and sharing openly with each other
in ecstatic celebration of MAKING?

While we understand and acknowledge the economic pressures and fear-mongering that
threatens to dominate and crush the creative impulse, we also believe that
now more than ever we have the tools to relinquish agency via cooperative means,
fueled by the fires of the Open Source Movement.

Looking out across the invisible vistas of that rhizomatic parallel country
we can begin to see our community beyond constraints,
in the place where intention meets
resilient, proactive, collaborative organization.

Here is a document born of that belief, sown purely of imagination and will.
When we document we assert. We print to make real, to reify our being there.
When we do so with mindful intention to address our process,
to open our work to others, to create beauty in words in space,
to respect and acknowledge the strength of the page
we now hold physical, a thing in our hand,
we remind ourselves that, like Dorothy:
we had the power all along, my dears.

THE PRINT! DOCUMENT SERIES
is a project of
the trouble with bartleby
in collaboration with
`the operating system`